CW00858903

Selenomania

Poems about Love, Loss & Life

By

Nathaniel Lloyd Richards

Contents

Introduction

Selenomania

Adjective (Selenomaniac)

1. *A person having an uncontrollable obsession with the moon*

2. *The moon having a direct effect on a person's mood and emotions*

Hopefully the above definition has made the title of this, my book of personal poetry a hell of a lot clearer! About the title, even as a child I had a deep obsession with the moon and would often sit and stare at it for hours and feel a sense of ease and release, nothing's changed. Growing older I've always liked the idea that whether it be me as a person or a relationship I've been a part of no matter what changed the moon was still always there, always constant, always the same.

Coincidently when gathering together all the Poems new and some older for this book I noticed I often mention the moon and so the title came to be. Another coincidence was that each chapter ended up consisting of 30 Poems each which I saw as a sign as I had recently turned 30 and I'm corny like that!

The book is separated in to three chapters the first being **Love** the good and the bad kind.

Secondly there is the chapter **Loss** recalling all those mixed emotions you get when it all goes bad and all that wine you consume in the process. Ha!

Lastly the closing chapter is **Life** which consists of Poems I've written about getting to know myself as a person, my relationships with friends and family, the loss of loved ones and my hopes for the future.

I hope you enjoy! It's been an emotional experience so if you don't, don't tell me! Ha

Nathaniel

Chapter 1

Love.

Misty Moon glow

What say the moon?

It stares down upon me and you,

Wondering,

As we do what's to become of us,

Pondering will it be victory or loss for our hearts,

He glares,

I briefly stare back shooting wishes and hoping he will grant me them back,

Who knew the moon could be so comforting?

Tonight it's glow feels warm as the sun as strange as it seems the misty
moon he looks over us observing and noticing two lovers at a cross road,

Neither knowing which road the other chose,

Here standing nose to nose underneath moon glow,

I wonder,

We wonder,

The moon it wonders,

Where do we go from here?

The Mafia

Nose in his book I'm his biggest fan,

"I'm gonna change the fucking world" is his master plan,

I don't doubt it,

Bursting to explode with ebullient creativity I envy,

Swoops up his guitar to casually serenade me,

That addiction to coffee and weed I'll let slide,

Because with him by my side,

Forget about it,

I would stand up in court and I would lie for you this you know,

I'm devoted to him like any Mafioso Capo,

I took a blood oath aimed my heart at you,

Ran the streets to let the whole city know that I'm devout to you,

For you I'd pull any trigger and fire,

I'm loyal to you just like The Mafia.

Runaway

You're not so easy to figure out a puzzle the greatest minds would debate about,

Your choices I admit are questionable yet you shrug them off with breezy nonchalance,

And I'm not overly confident but with you my fears evaporate,

On paper our situation seems like impending disaster,

Yet we drown the naysayers out with our abandoned laughter,

Your youth may be detriment to our longevity but you taught me to stop foreseeing and to let it all just be,

But sometimes worries come over me like that time we ran into the Floridian sea,

Now I'm as ready as I will ever be,

You tell countless lies but I see your truth and though we fight let it simmer,

I can feel the hope it glimmers,

Maybe I'm your faux patriarch and my advanced years are what entice you or maybe it's just that I don't want you to make the mistakes that I did too,

And though those I love would rather me stay away I'm drawn to you more with each passing day,

The stars are aligned let's run away,

Remember Birdland in Manhattan?

You held my hand under the table I know I'm strong but I was not able to stop the tingles they were irrepressible,

Though you claim to love Jazz I had an incline you only said it to appease me but that's ok I'm not too much into Musical theatre I only said I was because I thought I outta,

You love attention you strive for it,

It's your demon it dictates every single thing you do,

My feelings always come second best in the scheme of things I've gotten used to it for now it seems,

Still sometimes apprehensions take a hold of me,

But I'm pretty sure I'm ready now so let's just let this be,

Come and runaway with me.

Dickhead

His kisses feel like dying,

I should hold back trust me I'm trying,

But he seeps into my skin,

Feel him creeping around within,

Should have stood my ground and not let him back in,

He's a dark sickness of mine,

A poison of my usually perceptive mind,

He makes it so easy to hate him but so much easier to love.

I'll wait

I'll wait,

Time has taught me patience,

Please don't hasten,

I'll make myself comfortable,

'Cause I think you're worth it and the wise don't rush,

Rushing is for those who are apprehensive and unsure,

Not I,

I've known for a while,

I'll wait.

He bears no scars

He bears no scars his soul is immaculate no tears form in his eyes I guess he's just fortunate,

Whereas I feel the torment from his semi affectionate stance wondering why he won't fully let go and give this thing a chance,

He's my saviour but at the same time the cause for my despair half of me wants him to leave but the other needs him to be there,

Sometimes I appear cold towards him acting like I don't care when my heart and head know that I actually care more than I'd like to share,

My friends called a crisis meeting and it was said that they needed their Nae back I reply with I'll be fine again just once he shows he loves me back,

They sigh and say that they have heard that many a time,

I cry because I've actually kept count of the numerous times,

He bears no scars but they've suffused my weary body now he stays grounded firmly whilst I float off into a state of confused heart ache wondering why he does this,

Asking myself repeatedly why do I waste my love on somebody who doesn't grasp it,

And then it dawns on me he bears no scars because for me he does not care that's why he feels no penitence for I was just something to pass the time a hobby of sorts I guess it makes sense he was never in to sports,

I'm just trying to find the humour in this situation because knowing I've been wasting my life away waiting for his feelings to mirror mine is a fact that makes all my hope in love and life diminish triple time

And then there was you...

And then there was you,

Awkward yet charming you,

Popped up out of the blue with that silly hat and your one pair of jeans,

Sneaked up on me and enraptured my mind,

Posh boy Hip hop head with a penchant for weed,

I fell so hard I cracked the tiles on your kitchen floor,

Lay there peacefully as you'd make me bacon and pancakes galore,

Fun times like my cousin's party us dancing like liquored up fools,

The Lianne La Havas gig acting soppy and uncool,

And though we no longer speak you don't pick up at all,

I remember I was frozen once not interested in loves call,

And then there was you.

Fucking doubt

Peel away the question marks clinging to the sentences you speak,

We can take it easy there's no need to be so deep,

Kick me off my high horse and let's just lay here in the earth,

It's fine to be cautious but at times I over compensate,

I can see you slowly nodding so I know you can truly relate,

Pick me up gently and kindly put me in your pocket like keys,

I can bring you to your knees and open you up like you wouldn't believe,

That could be perceived as crude but just take it as you please,

Things don't have to be so intense let's relax and ride it out,

This could be fun if we let it let's say fuck you to doubt.

He's lovely

He's lovely,

He doesn't know he is but he is,

I don't know many other boys who would put up with me the way he does but he does, he really does,

I agree with what my critics say I'm damaged goods but it's ok he's here with his first aid kit in tow to cure me of the damage inflicted by those who came before,

So yeah, we're good,

He's lovely, the loveliest in fact and I feel blessed that he loves me, even at times when I get riled up start losing my temper talking that Mancunian slanguage he's not one to leave me to languish, all because…

He's lovely, I'm sure he has his nagging doubts about me but something inside him tells him I'm worth it,

 I've never been more humbled and I'm not a religious person but I really feel blessed to have him flanked up beside me even when cloudy tears prevent me from seeing I feel his presence omnipresent and all seeing,

Yes, I'm good all on my own but with him I'm a force to be reckoned with, it makes the stormy days easier to face to know what he thinks of me, simply because

He's lovely.

Future

We know how the story goes you bend but I break and shatter into a million trillion pieces,

Take off with the next rising wind until you come to your senses,

Scour the world and painstakingly put me back together again,

Then we start from the sweet beginning convinced there'll be no end,

Ignoring warning signs both fingers in our ears around our friends,

Seems everybody is a clairvoyant these days but I can write the future at the flick of a page…

Find you again

Rationality crumbles into nothingness, my heart pauses when my baby touches me,

My mind is engulfed with skydiving fluttering thoughts of us together,
Even if I wanted to there would be no room to think of another,

My baby has eyes greener than the prettiest emeralds even more so then those who scorn and bathe in envious waters,

Though my bank account is empty indeed my lover is all I will ever need although others may try to feed me temptation my appetite is contently whet,

And I swear to all of the Gods that I'm even more enamoured than the first day we met.
If I am the sunlight, my baby is the stars at night I was falling for the longest time my lover gave me wings to enable flight,

If the angels come today and want to take me away I'd have to interject with "but I'm not ready yet",

If it means being apart then I choose to stay

When it's my time I'll make sure not even death can keep me away,

I'd move earth and stone,

Stumble home,

I'll come and find you again.

I love ya

I kick doors closed like I'm Bruce Lee, when we argue oh how these walls do quake,

You jump in your car and break the sound barrier as I pound a text in to my phone saying "It's a good job I love ya",

We'd be excellent Historians or maybe Archaeologists how we exhume the past to see who will get the last laugh,

It's a good job I love ya otherwise I'd be trying my hardest to forget you like I'd never met you,

Your deceitful eyes don't lie when you dabble with subpar acquaintances when you get shut out of my bed you search for other vacancies,

Shit, it's a good job I love ya otherwise what would we do?

Friends would have their way I'd keep the hell away from you,

It's so lucky I love ya, even though we hurt each other and at times you drive me crazy,

honestly

I

still

love

you.

This one's for you

We all have a past,

Other people we let hold our hearts for a moment in time,

Me more than most I mistakenly gave it away with such haste until I realised, snatched it back and walked away at a rapid pace,

There are finger prints on my glass heart that I just can't rub away,

But just take them as a reminder that they just were not worthy,

I'm putting my trust in you so let's see all that you can do,

I've written about an awful lot of boys but,

This one's for you.

Like I know what love is

I guess my lover craves a simple object of affection I've never been that way I'm a complicated so and so and I guess that's how the river flows I meander around these obstacles I don't do stress at all,

I figure he thinks that I don't care I didn't put up a fight I could have sworn I saw the light die in his eyes,

His concerns were not mine and so I didn't see it my responsibility,

My boy likes to jump out of planes on weekends but he fears the thought of being with me completely, oh the irony

My heart is dark, it's sullen and complicated all feelings have vacated but there's a drop of hope that still resides that grows and grows after time so don't give up on me just yet because deep down I need you to want me,

I want you to love me like I know what love is.

I told him to choose the easy option, somebody else that he likes less but is willing to sacrifice,

I never mean to be as cold as polar bears toes but oh, the chill of my soul just seeps out of me and freezes any love which is directed at me,

I'm a frosty bitch it's easy to see, but I know deep in my core there's part of me wanting more a side of me locked in my vaults by those untruths of the many boys who have come before.

No Hesitations

See I'm no stranger to disillusion it's a habitual circumstance I'd rather do without,

Can't remember when last I took any advice there is never any time for doubt,

I heard it said I was the prince of solitude well bring on the crown and when it crumbles to dust I hope that he'll stick around,

What's in your mind?

I wonder from time to time does it mirror what's in mine?

Boy this was some climb I almost reached the summit but then I changed my fucking mind,

Easy come, easy go I guess that's what they say,

I'm unruly and I'm complicated,

Feelings change and my interests start fading but if you're worth it,

If this is worth it,

Then there will be no hesitating.

I know all my love is for him

Bee's to a flower,

Night to day,

There's not much more that I can say,

I know all my love is for him,

Friends say I'm crazy say I am blind tell me to wake up and open my eyes,

But I'm gonna love him until the day that I die that's why I know all my love is for him,

When we are parted my heart sinks to depths I didn't know it could my joyous eyes change and begin to flood,

I swear I know all my love is for him,

I've created our own little world away from the naysayers who nag and bitch like little girls,

I don't care for what they have to say it's my life it's up to me and who am I to argue with my heart,

I knew this right from the start,

That all my love is for him.

CoffeeWeedNightCap

I was going to walk through the meadows today the sun is shining and it somehow seemed like the perfect idea,

But fear of being alone with my thoughts stopped me I just don't want to think about you anymore so I will do laundry and all that boring stuff to keep my mind busy,

A week ago you smoked a spliff lay on me and told me I was gorgeous I remember casually thinking how could I ever want more than this?

I heard it say those who chase everything walk away with nothing at all but you still insist on chasing otherworldly perfection and I don't want to be the one to burst your bubble, so I won't call, I won't txt,

I think you need to see for yourself just what is out there but know I still care and I know it may not be physically but I am there if you need me just you say the word,

We both like jazz so if I call you my nightingale I've no doubt you will get the analogy if I'm hurting you then take this as my solemn apology

I know I have made the right decision and yet every night I'm haunted by your ghost rolling up at the end of the bed with that soft moon light on your face,

I memorised your routine it went bath, coffee, weed nightcap then embracing me like you do,

How I loved it when you called me boo,

Yes, it's the end and it's so fucking mundane but I liked how we started all the same.

Three Stars

There are 3 stars they run up my left arm,

Not for aesthetic reasons,

They represent three people who keep my heart beating,

At times we may disagree,

They may get angry at me,

I may say things I rarely mean in the heat of everything,

Yet even when I'm low they always say or do something that makes me giggle no matter how unwilling I may be they are all so equally silly,

I have 3 stars on my arm they strengthen me each day,

So when I feel like I can't go on I look to how they shine and it inspires me to thrive for my time,

We've been through things people our age shouldn't have had to endure but I guess that's what bonds us four together forming a force unbeatable,

When people look down their nose at the 3 stars on my arm it doesn't mean a thing to me because I know what they represent,

Tasha, Kysh and Lexi, all three mean so much to me.

Let's hang

You know me, I've got dead daddy issues that's my fucking problem,

I know you, you've got drugs in your history that's your fucking problem,

And I ain't out here to solve them but if you grow up soon maybe we can hang,

Let's go back in time to Brooklyn bridge in the summer time,

Watching the sunset behind the NY skyline,

And I don't want a lover I just need that friend of mine,

Let's go back to clear water beach baby let the cascading water wash all the pain away what do you say?

Let's hang, hey Hay, let's hang

You know me, I don't hold grudges that's not part of me,

And I think I know you so I'm hoping you do the right thing,

Gimme what I'm owed so we can move on that's what I want, and I know I've got people in my ear saying you just ain't no good,

That you're taking me for a ride and you are no friend of mine so don't you prove them right make it all clear like the stars that night we lay on the ground and I showed you the constellations

Took you awhile but I was patient and I want you again to call me 'your Nathan.'

River Phoenix

You smell like cheap cider, cigarettes and sadness my dark tortured soul of a boy come close let me hold you any heartrending situation we can strive through, I know you're broken I can fix you,

They say you're trouble you're no good but they don't know you like I do they don't see all the different colours of you, I do,

I see all of you the good, the bad, the insufferable and I love it all you're an addiction of mine, you drink too much, smoke too much, swear like a mother fucking trooper you do,

You have a wondering eye which is fine by me just as long as your eyes look back again to find mine,

I've heard it said that people don't change, who said that? I hate that and I tend to disagree with that point of view because I have a whole lot of faith in you

Oh your love is dangerous you're so unpredictable yet I don't care about how much he hurt you and all that other shit just shut up and kiss me hard be my River Phoenix

I smell like cheap cider, stellar and lies, I've been lying to myself this isn't me, drinking in the park after dark this is so alien to me, but I wanted to visit your world I want to be close to you, you unruly, unpredictable beautiful boy,

 I'll follow you down this road of self-destruct hoping you see the light, I was told to walk away but that's something I'm not prepared to do,

my own private bad boy only you shall know,

Just how much you fill my days with both sadness and joy.

Fire

There's a deep quiet set about us,

My mind is racing swinging this way and that way,

You're still dripping wet from the shower you just left I try to concentrate watch the beads of water race down you,

And I'd like to embrace you just like I knew you'd suggest but the heart is a muscle and mine needs its rest,

Try to distract myself reading local papers but stolen petty change and missing pets just don't have the desired effect,

When you kiss my neck I melt through the ceiling and say to myself

"Man, I've missed this feeling"

Three years of friendship and just like that we can snap back like my fucking hat,

I hate that I'm powerless when it comes to you it will always be you and I guess that is that.

Blink

We sat on the tables in that candle lit bar as the band played a Billie Holiday song,

I talked about my love for her but stopped myself as I felt my story went on far too long,

You gently grab my hand smile and tell me to carry on,

I blink and when I open my eyes we are two-stepping to hip hop in your living room,

I followed you to the kitchen when you spun around and kissed me,

I blink once more, open my eyes to us at breakfast you giggled at my clumsiness and I sunk in my chair,

You talked about your weekend plans and how you'd like me there,

Three months disappeared before I even noticed them approaching this is where the story ends I don't ever address the end,

I do wonder still if you ever listen to Billie though and get even slightly upset,

Reflecting on that bar and on the first time we ever met.

Or else we'll never know

Let me lay you down in my room nothing but a sound,

My eyes burrow into you and I tour your imagination, whisper secrets into my keen ear and as they seep into me I will hold them here dear,

Breathing synchronised as we muster the power to freeze time,

I could be anywhere but here is the place I'd longed to be cars race outside bark as they pass by and I see through the blinds a crescent moon casually observing,

I don't care at all who he's seen you with before, locked in an intimate gaze, my full heart anticipates

If we lay here forever nothing can bring us down we could work this out,

If we stay here together we won't fall apart delve into my heart,

Because even if the sun crashes down and the world comes to an end we will last forever, our love is for forever, just lay here with me, don't let me go or else we will never know.

I sat down last night with my insecurities and I told them this wasn't working out,

I couldn't let the ghosts of those you'd been with before stop me from ever wanting more so I slowly frog marched my nagging doubts to the front door and locked them out, so hush now don't explain in the background Billie Holiday asks "what is there to gain?"

All I saw in our future was pain thoughts making me go insane,

So now I'm solely fixed on us and what we can be happiness seemingly unending I'm done with all the silly pretending.

Wishing

Our relationship is so unstable like a ship sailing uncertain waters our hearts inside crashing around the captain's quarters,

We are like a light switch one minute we're off then the next we're on there's no in between when it comes to you and me,

We fuss, we fight, make up all night, and in the morning wake up together but still so far apart we've got hurting each down to an art,

We both know exactly what to say to cut each other deeper than ever before till our love for each other is limp and lifeless on the floor,

Then we patch it up help it to recuperate then every thing's great until the next time one of us so much as breathes the wrong way,

We war whilst playing 'Call of duty' too worked up to notice the irony,

You scream at me and I yell back step outside of my body to observe the scene, so ugly, it makes the wounds in my heart deepen,

We love each other still but I guess maybe too much, passion is overrated it causes too many problems,

But still I have one small hope that you and I can solve them,

We rise, we fall, never remain constant, I have travel sickness just trying to keep this going,

One minute we're like the poster couple for a blissful relationship then the next we're spiralling into the relationship graveyard,

And it's at that point that I revert to my inner child, fingers crossed, Head to the sky,

Just wishing that this shit works out this time.

You

Can we lay?

Lay here until the sun rises then we'll watch it sullenly fall again,

Can we lock eyes, doors and hands?

Shut the world out for the whole weekend,

Then on Monday we'll both call in sick and dive back into bed quick,

I think we've watched these films a thousand times,

Listened to this Shangri-Las song a thousand times,

I don't care it still feels fresh with you here,

And when you sing that adlib which is kinda off key I don't mind because it's you,

And you know I have a keen ear for melody,

You know me well,

I hate love,

I hate people,

I hate pretty much every damn thing but you.

Still Waters

Still waters lay undisturbed that's you and how you'd prefer to stay whilst I, I'm a river running wild never afraid of what lies beyond the bend,

We are two conflicting personalities here stands me bold and unwary and there you go Mr. rational,

I follow my first instincts and you debate over potential outcomes,

Let's be frank we're from two different worlds I'm alien to you, you sometimes don't understand the things I say and do,

But deep inside of you lies intrigue because in a way our differences make us similar,

I can't put down in words what I'm really trying to say but I'll try anyway because I feel it a waste to just let you walk away knowing that we both will bare regret even though we won't say,

So why can't we take things day by day the future will come when it comes and we'll deal with it that day,

The end of us can't come about just because things are working out,

Run free with me just like wild horses do who cares about labels it's just about me and you,

Whatever will be will be but for now I don't see why fear should stop something that was perfectly good to me,

Still waters lay undisturbed but sometimes it takes a pebble thrown by someone who sparks your interest to change it all and in turn create a waterfall.

Pinocchio Boy

I have splinters in my fingertips because your heart is wooden and I foolishly handled it,

I thought that I could change it into flesh and blood but my attempts were futile, it just would not budge,

I thought I could show you how real love would feel hoping you would embrace it and so break the seal,

Because when you let love in there is no going back your heart has longing for it, that is fact,

But still you wouldn't entertain the thought of the only four letter word that you feared becoming a part of you,

So you shunned any humanistic qualities which could be misleading as to the fact that your heart is even beating,

It's rigid I see, I have pencils with more feeling than you and I'm just being real,

I'm breaking my back here and you don't seem to see,

My Pinocchio boy, you don't know how to feel, my Pinocchio boy, you don't know what's real,

I pray one day you'll be able to feel real emotions,

Because currently I just can't see a you and me because you don't know what love is you don't know it's wonder,

How it makes your heart tremble like thunder,

My Pinocchio boy open up and let love flood in.

Ungodly reason

For some ungodly reason we just can never get right at times we soar so high and I love it but when we crash back to earth I fucking hate it,

We've had so many failed attempts we're the relationship Tim Henman and I don't want us to walk away no victory to show for,

Friends they say to me "Nae, you really can't stay" and I say to them I know I mustn't but at the same time something inside says I must,

The God's they tend to hate us and so they continually bate us we lay at the hands of their mercy like pawns on an otherworldly chessboard,

I want to move forward but I don't want to harm you,

I want to disarm myself but also don't want to be laid vulnerable for you, That'd be too easy and so I keep my cards close to my chest I learnt from the best,

For some ungodly reason our relationship breezes through seasons the warmth of summer to the bitter icy cold breath of winter, it all gets too much for me and my poor little heart sometimes,

We struggle on bruised and battered but yet still unshakable defiant even, For some ungodly reason the God's don't want us to succeed and so they make our love a tragedy, make us an example put us on show for them all to bleed,

I'm re-reading all the love stories I own seeing if I missed this part it's funny I don't remember a book I read where love was this hard,

At least Romeo and Juliet met their end so deep in love whereas this constant back and forth with us makes me not so quite sure,

For some ungodly reason we've been resigned to this fate and I just hope that we can turn the tables on us before it's all too late.

No good

Hold me close like I am yours and I'll pretend we're more than friends,
Stroke my hair like you always do so I can act like it's only me and you,

I'll stay the night like I always do and we'll do things like lovers do,

Just this once I'll pretend he's not more handsome than I nor a nicer person to,

I'll play the role of the one you love until the sun comes up and you freeze up, before you push me away make me feel this is my fault let me stay here for a while in your arms like a child,

I'm no fool I know my place but a boy can dream and so I play out this scene,

You don't like a challenge I've seen this now and as he is the easy option I'll just bow out,

You tell me you care about me but I'm not so quite sure because if you really did I'd feel it when we kiss,

Sometimes I start to wonder should I be flattered that it's always me there are other boys who'd jump to be in my position hotter boys than little old me,

But I don't see it as a compliment really because you always go back to him,

I have you for just one night the other days belong to him,

If only the nights were longer so I could still pretend that you don't just hang around with me because the sex is good and maybe I'm babbling and being misunderstood, I guess I'm trying to say being second best is no good.

J

Fuck it, I dig you, you intrigue me I'm curious,

I like how your eccentric mind takes our conversation to weird and exciting places so sporadically it's baffling but it peaks my interest,

I'd had it with guys who were real life colour photo copies of those who came before, oh what a bore,

Tell me about genocide again, teach me Yiddish if you like I'm interested in your culture,

Let's once again be a gross contradiction and go and drink £2 cider in the park whilst we discuss religion and education sort out the world like it's our occupation,

I'm desperately trying to play it cool and not mess this up because it's rare I meet someone who can keep up with my random tendencies,

You change the colour of your hair as much as I do, no that's no indication that I should be with you it's just a flippant observation but all the same one I really like,

J won't you stay and toast the ridiculous stereotypes that surround us,

You think like me, I think like you, so raise your glass let's point and laugh,

I like you, I know it's early days but I like you,

J it's ok you can stay we don't have to do a thing we can sit in my conservatory get really drunk and sing along to Amy,

That sounds like fun, so what do you say?

I wanna kiss you so badly J, say that's ok?

Chapter 2

LOSS

Same Moon

Different country but that's the same moon,

That's the same moon that led me to you,

Different year but that's the same moon,

That's the same moon who silently watched us argue,

Its mares look different but we've changed too,

You've changed the most, the old you an omnipresent ghost,

I left without a goodbye because you did your very best to make me cry,

So I did what all night birds do,

Aimed for the moon and took to the sky.

The Breakup

Your hand in mine,

The silence makes my brain implode,

As time makes my patience erode,

You smile half-heartedly as is a regular occurrence with you lately,

It smacks me right on my cheek as if done physically,

My knee's they tremble as they did at the beginning but this time the reasoning couldn't be any more different,

I choke on the words as I ask you "where's this going?",

Your eyes they fall so just the top of your head is showing,

The silence revisits us until the clocks ticking becomes deafening,

Whilst inside my chest I feel my heart deflating,

In my hand I hold the last spark of us it's flickering dying painfully,

I hold it close to my body in the hopes it will survive this evening,

And your phone is beeping, it's irritating, whoever it is doesn't know just what they're interrupting,

Cause this could be the end of something I truly thought was beautiful,

Sadly, I see that I was alone in this thinking, we're sinking, there were obviously faults like White star boats but I Just didn't know, or maybe I did but chose to ignore them in hopes they'd float away,

But now as I sit here today and watch you slowly but gradually fall out of love with me,

I wish I'd have taken heed, admitted defeat,

Because it's excruciating to tell someone you'll love them forever for them to turn around and say that that's not on their agenda,

So as our hands slip their grasp and I bare my palm to see the chain I once bought you that simply spelled out 'Love',

I realise the end has come,

And what I thought was ever lasting is finally done.

Heartbreak food

Note to myself I mustn't stick my earphones in and listen to sad songs of
love's gone wrong,

I must leave that full bottle of vodka in the bottom of the fridge,

I won't cry myself to sleep tonight I won't resort to that,

And though I feel so lonely here half way across the world I won't feel sorry
for myself I won't spell it out in my Facebook status,

I won't get mad, I won't get even, I refuse to be depressed although I'm
slipping into that territory I won't let it consume me,

I may eat a lot of shit like cosmic brownies, lays potato chips and a full
bottle of 69¢ strawberry pop followed by a whole tub of ice cream but I'm
cool with that,

That's standard heartbreak food, It's kind of like my therapy,

I hate what you have done to me but you I just can't hate, cause no matter
how much your words cut me they still can't cut our bond and although the
blows of misery rain down upon me constantly these snacks they cushion
the impact and comfort me so handily,

I guess that's why they call it convenient food because it's so easy to digest
when you're feeling blue,

I'm not even thinking about my waistline it can triple if it so pleases cause
all I really care about is not crumbling to pieces,

If you don't want me anymore, then I'll raid the nearest store, stuff my face
till my stomachs sore and hope I won't feel this hurt anymore.

Neil/Silent refrain

My boy has a mouth on him,

Reel it in I just can't,

A tongue even more brash and loose than mine,

He's complicated roots as deep as the Oceans and Seas,

I was struck and enamoured when his love washed over me,

He screams at me till we both cry,

I storm out walk the long way home find him standing in my hall,

He makes me feel bipolar how my moods feel so unbalanced,

My baby is unpredictable I guess that's why now when I call out his name,

I receive a silent refrain.

Nothing's the same

Though I smile, though I laugh, though I function as before and show not one chink in my stainless steel facade,

Nothing's the same,

Though we've stayed friends and can go for meals you'd probably think when I ask how he is that I'm already completely healed,

No. Nothing's the same,

When it rains and you are not here I simply wonder the streets just to see if I still feel,

You have no idea, I've never allowed you to see but one tear, when friends ask if I'd like to go to my favourite bar and I kindly decline they have no inkling why,

Because at times I get so good at tricking myself and almost always get away with it,

At times when my mother and sisters tell me I'm looking well and I say I feel it,

Those times when I say to my friends lets go out and laugh all night I almost forget that I'm not over you,

Nothing's the same, I fucking hate change, oh it's such a waste,

When we hangout now and you flirt like you used to do I retaliate with something sweet but sassy like I'm so nonchalant to it,

Act like you don't still make my heart skip and when you describe him and tell me how you're finally ready to settle down I hold my breath so you don't hear me sigh,

Smile so hard it's impossible for me to cry,

Silences that were atmospheric before now have a stinging taste of awkwardness,

So I crack a joke to lighten the mood just like I used to do but nothing ever stays the same, funny how now you can finally word how you truly feel.

Supa Dupa Fly

Home girl's fucking with Marc again I know how this shit will end,

I remember I was foolish once,

Pray remember me as I am not how I was,

Thinking rationally is my new favourite trick,

Unless it's a day when my mouth is slick,

Please let that slip,

I grew up a care free flower child,

Though no flowers grew out of that concrete ground,

I was technicolour in this grey city,

Remember when I was messing with Neil?

I say messing it felt real,

We'd argue about the most irrelevant things,

He disagreed with my choice of favourite Missy album which would turn to him saying "Well get the fuck out then",

I used to rise to it all before but now I'd simply leave it for the birds,

My mother warned me about heartache and what it does to the soul,

So now I'm cautious before I serve my raw heart whole.

Matty

Shoot me dead if I'm guilty of caring,

I guess your misery was so voluminous you felt like sharing,

I cried last night from the words you said,

Woke up lay upon a floating bed,

A glimmer of positivity clinging to me,

The only wrong I did was to give a fuck,

Until you decided you'd had enough,

Don't txt, don't call, leave me alone,

I'm not used to boys who are nice and all,

Your words made no sense but you spat them with such fire,

I rolled over and closed my eyes,

Turning my back on my stupid desires.

DWL (Down with Love)

The notion of having to grasp love before it fleets is currently escaping me,

Let me make things clear so there is no chance of mistaking me,

I think love is a beautiful thing for those who seek it but from experience I realise once you invite it in the door is left ajar for its friends to come in tow,

There's misery, pain and Mr. Irrational,

So the last time love tricked me into a heavily veiled sense of security and then waited till I was down on the ground to unleash its final blow to me,

I finally pulled myself back to my feet and made a vow to myself that it just wasn't for me,

Me and love we have issues no counselling could cure,

If there are undeniable riches in love than I'd rather just go poor,

Fools in love act like they can fly so it's hilarious to me when I see them take a leap and fall in piles all around my feet, if only they could see how pointless love is,

They say that it can last forever but I'd like some proof,

I mean people can stay together forever but is that love or convenience? Romance isn't dead that comes at the start or when things aren't at their best,

It's used to hide the cracks which every loving relationship has, I can be called cynical but I'd prefer a realist and at the end of the day I only have my hearts feelings at interest.

When I go

When I go mountains will crumble,

Rivers won't flow,

The sun won't rise,

Not even tears will cascade from your frozen eyes,

Angels will fall from the skies become mere mortals and eventually die,

This all sounds so dramatic I know but when I go,

You'll fall slow,

Everything you thought was constant will go,

Then at least you'll know.

Cruel for sport

You're cruel for sport, have that shit down to an art,

It feeds your already over indulged ego to watch me cave in to myself right before your eyes when you spear me with words dripping with poisonous intent,

My strength all spent no longer able to fight for change, completely outmatched in this dangerous game,

You're cruel for sport simply because you can, I never object I just choose to deal with the side effects,

And oh how it drains each day is a chore when you strike me with one of those deadly blows without even touching me,

The bruises that are inflicted on me they run so incredibly deep I call my best friend but whimper so much I can't speak,

She's so angry at me right now and I can't say I blame her she calls me a fool and a glutton for punishment calls our setup another form of self-harming and I say "charming",

But inside not completely disagreeing because I'm finally seeing the light in me is fleeing,

You're cruel for sport at my expense and it's a damn shame because I love you all the same,

I stare into you sometimes and search for signs of guilt but I guess that's just not the way you were built because all I can see staring back at me is unwavering resentment for what I'll never know all I know is,

You're cruel for sport so I guess letting you win is my last resort.

Christmas Day

Here you go again,

Trying your best to antagonise me,

You know my temper burns a wicked red,

Tempting it to bare its ugly head,

I got tired of waiting,

So when you show up to the house 3 hours late,

I see your eyes scan the room for a dinner plate,

Nope,

Not today and sorry you can't stay been waiting on your ass like Christmas
day.

The Birds

The birds are gleefully singing extra early this morning and their tune which usually perks me up is making me want to throw something to shut the motherfucker's up,

Last night's words you threw at me are burnt into my skin like raw tattoo's, Wicked words who's only aim was to cause me pain a fact I hope you are ashamed, my throat is sore from yelling and the tears I cried whilst asleep have turned to dust upon my cheeks,

Who would have thought I'd be here at this point where the venom I feel for you can't be topped, I loved you more than life itself I really did, yes I really did,

So why now when I think of you today does my gut wrench and I get short of breath? We flipped 180° on each other baby any love we had is more than faded, I look at you as a mistake I made like a life lesson of which I didn't get the grade,

What started as a civil conversation turned to a war of words and now my scars are evident and you were like "yeah, whatever then"

But my heart was stone and crumbling not knowing what was happening you were stood in front of me morphing into somebody I've never seen before,

 Your old soul seeped out of you and was writhing on the floor, and I was rowing with a stranger with a familiar face, who with every phrase he made was slowly destroying me,

So as I lay here this morning still wishing death upon those birds I painfully begin to realise I really didn't know you at all.

Blow it

I wish you knew me,

I wish I knew you,

If we knew each other like we tried to pretend you would know how to
address me,

I'm crazy,

I've made peace with that fact, I just need you to know it too so we don't
have any problems,

I'm unsure of your decisions in life and how it's destined to go,

Not completely confident in any person's decision to let a boy like me go,

I've got my shit in check,

I fend for myself,

Pretty from the soles of my feet to the follicles on my head,

Educated, distinction graded in bed,

Funny as shit and you damn well know it,

Oops look at that!

Why'd you have to go and blow it?

Starbucks

I've been unable to sleep baby been drinking all through the night lately, I've never felt so alone,

I go to stroll through the busiest shopping centres and malls just so I don't feel so on my own,

I've forgotten how to smile so I look into the faces of strangers having a good time to remind myself of how to do it,

I hear your voice bounce off the walls inside my head when I lay awake in bed,

So I roam the deserted streets and roads to wear my mind out and shut you out,

Most of the time I'm so mundane but I sometimes flip out and cry, throw things, like the picture of us the frame I've had to replace on multiple occasions,

Don't fear for me though every other aspect of my life is doing fine I just lose myself and get hung up on you sometimes,

I get a pain when someone mentions your name glaze over so they don't see how much it hurts to be reminded of you not being around,

I try to speak but my voice box doesn't produce a sound,

I smile and nod blinking back the tears so they change the subject as I watch them vow to themselves never to make that same mistake again,

My best friends call now and then asking me if I want to go out with them and part of me would like to, but part of me just wants to sit here and cry too,

I sit in Starbucks and sip on coffee,

I don't even like the stuff but its busy,

The noise drowns out your voice and I can pretend with all these people around that I didn't come here on my own,

I get the bus home alone there's empty seats but I sit next to someone, comforted by the company,

I walk the long way to my house avoiding my empty home as much as I can, put the telly on even though I'm not watching it and pretend the voices are people keeping me company,

I miss you.

Gin & Fiona Apple

I drink Gin and listen to Fiona Apple,

Friends and family sadly just can't relate,

Advice they give makes me so irate,

This breakup is too tough to grapple,

My demons and insecurities challenge me to a wrestle,

I'm outmatched,

What happened to us?

I feel like I was the sole one to be in the dark,

Until your actions shined a light on the whole sad affair,

Now even the simplest of tasks is so trying,

So I drink Gin and listen to Fiona Apple when I feel like dying,

Then I feel ok,

I'm not completely healed yet but for now I'm ok.

Again

I was left alone in the dark again,

So I called up Caroline and hit the town again,

She said what's wrong and I lied again,

She asked me once more with that knowing tone again,

I told her my heart was torn again,

She gave a knowing nod and went to the bar again,

I texted Joey to see how he was again,

He knew from just a text I was blue again,

He took a train to my town to give me those harsh truths I need again,

Dionne said it best when she said "Nae he's a knob"

I tell myself this when my heart gets crushed again,

When over the rainbow is too far it's best to grab best friends and hit your favourite bar (again).

Bartender

Bartender I do not want any kind of late night therapy please just pour me a drink if you would be so kind,

My problems are exactly that mine and mine alone so if I choose to put them in a box and use that same box as a bar stool as I casually drink them away that's my choice entirely,

Pour me something strong I don't drink it usually but I hear whisky is the one if you want to get drunk quickly,

So poor me, pour me a glass like my first name is Buck I come from Tennessee and I just don't give a fuck,

Mixers are for pussies I'll have mine on the rocks, self-made amnesia is my one true aim will you be my accomplice that's all I ask?

Will you ignore the tears that now and then fall and disturb the liquid within my glass?

Let's just pretend I'm fine like I'm not rotting from the inside out, if you don't ask questions and just keep pouring I promise to tip you well I'm half cut already so currently it'd seem like money well spent.

I will sit right here until my problems disappear well at least until my eyesight and foresight are so blurry I no longer see them here, this bar is now home I don't want to go to my own,

That's where my demons are waiting to greet me and I don't want them bastards to defeat me, so Bartender do me a favour fill it up and don't ask questions please I'm alright it's just one of those nights forgive me whilst I dwell in my woefully unwavering plight.

Swiftly

Swiftly, your love went so swiftly,

I blinked but I did not see,

You suddenly walk away from me,

Oh and the loved dripped away swiftly,

Swiftly, I held on tight but you slipped away from me,

You walked away into the summer breeze,

I saw you fade into the gang of Sycamore trees,

I begged you to stay but you carried on your own way,

And you walked away so swiftly from me.

If we never speak again

Why does it hurt so bad after all this time? Nothing pains as bad as no reply,

I walk to our old haunts feeling the environments taunts songs in my ears we used to play in your tiny box room every day,

I drown myself in drink on lonely nights wake up swimming through tears then hate myself for being so damn pathetic, my friends say this will only defeat me if I let it but what do I do now? No resolve I have no clue now,

I should pick myself up off this cold dirty floor coax myself into getting over you now, but how can I find myself and start a new when all my attention is focused on looking for you?

Thought my pride would overrule desperation but the desire to talk to you is overwhelming,

Walking past your old house I seldom do but the last time I did I saw me and you dancing around in your living room like we used to do,

I'm not afraid of many things, I'd swim leagues of oceans if I had to, climb the highest mountain if need be, but one thing I fear is if we never speak again, that's a pain I don't think I could comprehend.

I saw you through the crowd at the Mvula gig we locked eyes and you panicked and split whilst my gut received a swift unexpected kick,

So we can't even nod and say hello? Is this what we have now become?

I remember your smile and how you'd hunch when you were reading, I miss you but I doubt that you miss me too a thought that constantly has me reeling.

Déjà vu

These bitter tears taste familiar,

Me in the foetal position clinging to a box full of tissues reminds me of many times before,

The weathers changed and honestly I'm kind of glad to see the rain, Nothing's changed,

It always ends the same,

Once again I get bereft from love, deprived of those feelings I longingly crave it's all so familiar and feels exactly the same,

This isn't pain I'm feeling it's just déjà vu,

These nostalgic feelings strike a chord with me,

I've been here before and I was waiting for this to occur,

It's not hurt I feel, it's just déjà vu

At this point I'm an expert on failed relationships,

I seriously could write a book detailing how my love life is so majorly fucked up,

I just can't be surprised anymore I just expect this outcome because for me it's become the norm,

I anticipate, quash any optimistic hopes of this guy being 'the one' it's a defence mechanism and it's served me sufficiently.

Walking

I walked out mid argument as I just couldn't bare the screaming, I was choking on disdain for you and truly hating that feeling,

I grabbed my keys, my wallet and pride I walked until I was happily lost,

I didn't look back not even once to see if you were there, out of sight and out of mind I really did not care,

I purposely left my phone on the table didn't want you to call no not at all, cars violently roar at me as they rush by on this unfamiliar street,

I'm emotionally shaky but still I'm sturdy on my feet which aids this rapid pace of which I'm currently travelling,

Destination unknown as long as it isn't home I needed to flee so I could breathe,

Your spiteful ways had their foot on my oesophagus, you 've always been as stubborn as a spoilt hippopotamus we can't be in the same room right now it's damaging to my soul so stew in your own pot of fierce resentment and I shall return when I feel I can face it,

I flew out the door feet not touching the ground I zoned you out, the obscenities I just couldn't bear, who is that standing there with that unfamiliar glare?

I know that face I've dyed that ruby red hair but when you called me unlovable, unworthy and a bore I died thrice, this person I don't know him,

I turned on my heels and out the door I was walking to find my sanity, to a happier state of mind, subconsciously walking stupidly, to reverse time and go back to that place when we were fine.

Deal.

My man's gone now I told that boy he had to bounce the weight of how
many fucks I give? Not even half an Ounce,

Dyeing my hair a shade of 'Red wine' red for glory and to mimic what's in
this glass,

Told depression to kindly kiss my ass,

I'm set, I'm good, I'm emancipated, satisfied with the final words I launched
his way left him emasculated,

I'm good at that I excel he was shocked and unprepared I could truly tell, no
remorse from me he should have bothered to treat me well

If you really were the one I'd be sat here inconsolable,

If it was meant to be just you and me I would not be drinking Bacardi,

In the club,

No fleeting thoughts of doubt,

No missing my spouse,

Out with my friends,

And it's not like I need to get over you it's more the fact I struggle to
remember you,

Yep that's how I truly feel,

This resentment is so fucking real,

And you can just deal.

Stardust

I can see me swimming around inside your sparkling eyes I slice through the crystal blue waters at peace with the world,

As we lay entwined I feel that you are closely monitoring the time because deep inside you know that I never stay for more than just a day,

You grip me tighter subconsciously in hopes that I'd have no chance of breaking free, how silly, you knowing me know that I always find a way,

It's the downside of loving me I can commit to a certain extent but that kind of responsibility scares me, forces me to flee, you whisper you love me and at that exact moment I wriggle free,

leap to your window sill and as I shoot a last glance behind me I see that your head is already down, it's like even though you're used to me leaving you it doesn't make it any easier for you,

So as I soar like a rocket into the midnight sky I cover my ears tightly as not to hear you cry,

As I return to the sky, sparkling like stardust realising every attempt at sticking around for you always ends up bust,

I wish that I could love you more but your feelings frighten me so I spiral off into space to keep a safe distance, you know this by now, at least of all things I'm consistent,

you can see me up above shining just for you but know that I will never settle down on this earth for you.

Best thing you ever lost

Remember when you punched me in that bar and blacked my eye? You said you didn't expect that to happen, well shit, neither did I,

This sets the tone in a way to explain our relationship you'd throw emotional punches my way then stand back and admire the bruises,

But this time was physical and I knew I had three options,

I could have embraced my inner anger as you know it burns red retaliated as a reflex buried my pint glass in your head,

Or number two I could have let you leave then called them people on you have them kick down your door, that would be a problem,

But the option I chose was a decision I still stand for right there in that moment I said never no more, no I'm no angel but I knew for a fact that I deserved so fucking much more,

Though my eye may be black look closely you will see it has its sparkle back, free from you and the fucked up things you do,

No longer am I poisoned by your wicked mind games, watch my lips as they smile and they slowly whisper to you goodbye,

Good luck being alone, that's your destiny, good luck on your quest of replacing me, you will see,

The best thing you ever lost was me.

Tables turn

When I first met you, you were ten feet tall,

Now you're so small I can barely see you at all,

It's funny how the mighty fall those who seem invincible are probably the most fragile of all,

A voice once powerful, knowledgeable and booming now is a nervous whisper without any meaning,

And you said I was the lost cause with nothing to live for,

Your true colours are showing and low and behold they're not as effervescent as I once thought,

Your image is tainted and I'm positively glowing,

Treat those how you would wish to be treated I guess the true meaning of this is showing,

Who would have thought I'd be the one in control now that I'm finally going?

Sing

How do you heal?

How do you move on?

Sing.

How do you again begin to feel?

How do you carry on?

Sing,

You just have to sing.

Blue Elephant in the room

I see the side wards glances, hear the gentle lowering of tone,

Those who know me best can always sense my loneliness,

I see their darting eyes each encouraging the next to say what we're all
thinking,

Even when I'm out of line and rude they let it slide which is so unlike them,

If I was to explain in words how down and out I feel inside I think the
concern they'd feel for me would be too much to bear,

So out of love for those who care I keep it all there, inside, and I refuse to let
them see how huge the tears are that I only share with the night,

I'm pretty good at nonchalance have it down to a fine art, but when I briefly
escape into another room I have to gather myself and take a breather,

It's tough and I suspect that secretly they know what I'm doing, but for my
own piece of mind I'd like to at least try to show them that I can still be
strong,

The way I see it is there's nothing wrong with having pride and protecting
those you love,

It's best if the worst is left unspoken I'm just not ready to be that open.

Storm of heartbreak

I can hear it in the distance rapidly drawing near its thunderous and frightening so I cover my ears, I have a fear of precipitation storm clouds make my knee's tremble,

As you begin to talk I hear a rapturous thunder roar so I'm praying you will stop because this whole scenario is incredibly overwhelming my tear ducts are welling but just as my blue tears are about to fall I use all my might to prevent that occurrence,

Appear brave just to forsake you, stand my ground, the worst out comes swimming around my mind,

You continue to speak as a lightning bolt strikes just right outside, this was what I was trying to avoid every time you said we needed to talk,

I knew what the topic of conversation would be so I kept myself busy said I just didn't have the time right now, but now there's nowhere to run, nowhere to even hide, the thing that I've feared has finally cornered me,

we both know why you've come here, and as the words tumble out of your mouth, the dark clouds that have been stalking me finally let their rain drops free

Here it is, the storm of heartbreak I feared this day, prayed it wouldn't come even tried to run but the inevitable had to occur, so that is why I sit here soaked right through, head down, eyeing the ground,

I've finally started to cry not that you would know, it's hard to tell what's tears and what's rain streaming down my face, I leave and walk the long walk home, storm in tow, just to remind me that I'm now alone.

Stall

You sure have a lot to learn and I hope you don't end up getting yourself burnt, I could have been your teacher,

I'd have guided you well, we'd have had a ball but you had to make us stall, I think I pity you, because at one time I was where you are and so I know how hard you'll kick your future self for letting fear prevail and not taking a leap,

And it's not even that deep but it could have been but I guess it's my own thinking of what should have been,

That leaves this bitter after taste in this mouth of mine and makes me sometimes wish I could press re-wind,

Un-send that text kept it to myself but the honest truth is you'd have always found an excuse an easy get out card,

I guess I should have known this the signs were prominent,

And I've been second guessing pulling my hair out and stressing asking myself did I push it were you not ready and am I to blame?

But the fact is I went at your pace I let you lead, scene through scene, so when you mentioned the pressure I was taken a back and confused but the reality is the pressure comes from your quantum leaping into what could have been our future,

It rocked your soul and drove you cold but that wasn't my doing and yet you made it out like I was to blame, when I wasn't at all

So now as we stall probably for the final time I say goodbye to the what if's as I read your txt's that no longer bare a 'kiss'.

The blame

I class myself as a perceptive person but I guess for a while that part of my brain just wasn't working,

Because I thought I had you all figured out, I knew you well of that I had no doubt,

Now looking at how this all turned out, I could really just kick myself,

I take the blame,

For playing your game and it's a shame, we hang out as friends now and I see characteristics in you that are totally brand new I don't even think you know the real you,

Searching for an identity, at one time you were a clone of me and now you worship at his feet until the next guy you happen to meet,

I take the blame and of that I'm ashamed,

For not playing you at your stupid little game,

I thought we were on the same page when in fact we wouldn't even be classed in the same genre and things I still ponder like did you really care?

Were those moments ever real like when you'd gently stroke my hair?

Maybe I shouldn't even care, we crumbled to dust and I'm just waiting on that last final gust to blow it all away, hoping that not one iota of the emotions I felt for you will stay, and you can call me, yes you can stop by,

We can be civil, tell your family and friends I said "Hi" but as far as the love we shared,

My word has been spoken how could we have made it whole when we started off broken,

And yes I still take the blame, I should have been cautious,

I was older and more experienced but I guess I thought I'd seen it all, thought we were standing too tall together to ever even fall,

And now I pity the next guy who comes along my walls have been built tall and so fucking strong,

It'll take a while to bring them down but the guy who manages to do so he'll obviously be worth it,

He won't be like you when he says he loves me he'll mean it.

Chapter 3

Life.

The Moon

I was a quiet child, shy and soft spoken even a little morose at times,
shoulders round, head down, eyes nervously scanning the ground,

I was lost for a while,

Angry without reason,

Knew things beyond my years but never keen to relay them,

I was lonely,

I was blue,

Kept it inside so they never knew,

The anomaly of the family nobody really knew how to handle me,

So I looked to the moon and it settled my soul for that moment in the day I
genuinely felt whole,

What's more majestic than the moon?

The sun would slowly begin to rise that's when I'd sadly whisper,

"See you soon".

Secret place

I raced the wind to my secret place,

Fell to my knees and began to pray,

I sent a prayer to those above and asked them to rid disease from someone I loved,

I soaked the floor with desperate tears and burnt a candle so God would see me clearly,

I asked why him and why us?

When people out there are evil doers but have perfect health,

Even now I don't understand why would God separate us when we only just were behaving again like a father and children should be like,

How cruel of him to steal him away and still it hurts like an open wound it will not heal, the exact pain we all feel,

And they say it gets easier but I think that's just one of those things that people say to comfort you,

But I'd prefer if they didn't say anything at all because it's worse to be lied to and still I visit my secret place I imagine he's found it too and he watches over it for me so when I visit we are reunited,

We watch the river flow together,

Observe the ducks cleaning their feathers,

But still sometimes when he's not close I whisper to up above and ask those in the upper room why they took his life so soon.

On a loop

They were all quitters so I just couldn't relate,

I shed them with a quickness like they were excess weight,

Eternal 'Ground Hog day' with them I could never contemplate,

So I left them at Thompsons Arms and left my twenties there too,

Left them frozen in time like a technicolour film on a loop,

I watched old me die and the new me bloom,

I wonder if they ever changed I may never know,

Or if they ever plucked the courage to finally grow.

City rain

I love the city when it rains,

I match the rhythm of raindrops with my sporadic thoughts,

I follow rivers of dreams flowing down every street,

Wonder until I'm blissfully lost,

Chasing grey clouds whatever the cost,

I embrace the rain it reminds me that everything I feel is not a dream it's
real,

I'm tempted to touch every single blue drop,

There I go again trying to do too much,

I love the city when it rains,

I take a stroll to ease my pain.

Untitled

There might as well be the thick potent smell of magnolia in the air, strange fruit plucked and strewn everywhere,

I'm so blackened with anger I'm not on any colour chart,

That was a metaphor if you caught it well done, if you didn't you really need to awaken and catch up,

I thought progress had been made until I turn another page, flick to another channel, eyes burning and swelling with rage,

New York I love you but right now I'm so disheartened,

Florida has my heart but what about Trayvon's?

I get furious at times when I reflect on Ferguson,

I've got my hands up,

Not spinning,

I'm on that pavement bleeding out,

U.K what happened? When did this happen?

I'm on that beach with my lifeless son in my arms and I'm sick to my stomach,

I don't feel love in Paris right now just hurt and I fear for Syria, I cried bitter tears that night I read about what's happening in Africa,

The world is run by idiots and stupidity now has a voice,

The ignorance is deafening,

They say be patient, fuck being patient let's have this conversation.

Peanut Butter

I don't really want a box a box is kinda stunting,

My overall true stance in life is to say what the hell I'm wanting,

And I don't mind being misunderstood when they define it awkward,

If solitude is my closest friend then you bitches are just imposing,

I'd like to smile all day every day but I wasn't born a liar,

I have a blind rage inside of me ask my ex once I set all his shit on fire,

I'm not proud of this but admit it felt good so I shrug and wave off the guilt,

I once asked my mother why am I like this? She said "Son that's just the way you were built",

I'll piss on your box because I'm a rude motherfucker,

When it comes to me being defined don't compare me to another,

They say I'm Peanut butter because I'm caramel complected and a bit of a nutter.

God's gift

My name means God's gift but what does that mean to me?

Nothing,

Unless there is to be some drastic spiritual shift,

Does gift mean I belong to be given?

Like I should be wrapped up and tied with a red ribbon?

Am I supposed to live up to some high standard like I've been spiritually branded?

My name is a form of flattery from a religion that would close its doors on me,

God's gift is the meaning but I'm present not something to be presented,

And I belong to me so the truth is it's resented.

Fairground

Candy floss scent,

Fears all spent,

Screams galore,

Such a bore,

Spinning, shooting, escape the ground,

Life in circles, merry go round,

Nausea ensues,

Highs turn to blues,

Unpopular opinion but I fail to care,

I've never actually enjoyed this fucking fair.

Drink

Drink, I just need a drink,

Let's skip the clink just raise and sink,

Intentional amnesia is what I think,

Drink, where's my bloody drink?

Not that of the kids,

Nothing blue with a fizz with tons of rocks,

I like my liquor hard like I like my....

Drink, no I do not want to think,

Don't call my phone leave me the hell alone,

Jack and Jim I call my own.

Free to be

I had to lose my way to find myself but first I had to stop comparing myself to everybody else,

How do you know where's home if you never leave?

How do you know what's happy if you've never been?

I've a lot of questions it seems,

Hopefully I'll have all the answers soon,

I built the foundations of the new me on the rubble and ashes of who I was before,

I'm stronger that's for sure,

Still 5"11 but I walk much taller,

Still softly spoken but the things I say now sound like a roar when I talk,

I was near sighted but now I see way into my future,

I dive under the waves of doubt, smile instead of shout,

Dragged my insecurities out of the shadows and watched them die in the daylight,

Just need to feel loved like family and that'll do me, I'm easily pleased,

I love me now, I'm free to be loved.

Nostalgia Lane

Fuck all that nonsense I'd rather play Goldeneye, Nintendo is my first love there's no need to cry,

People take this love thing too seriously don't get me wrong I've met heartbreak on a dark lonely night that's when I turned my back on him and reverted to my inner child,

Now it's Mario and Luigi no other boys can appease me, I'll be power sliding round those corners like how I swerve these guys' advances,

No more second chances it's game over for me in the future I won't rule it out but for now no more stupid love for me,

You won't see me in the clubs I'm elusive these days, won't see me at any shows I'm reclusive these days,

But you can find me down there on Nostalgia lane, I will be wearing hi tops and my chunky gold chain,

Beat boxing to my boom box, hat to the back, revisiting the good old days evidently willing them back,

The only person I want to be responsible for is my 96' Tamagotchi and that is that, I don't have time for a relationship as a matter of fact

Too many trees to climb and streams to wade what's the use in a relationship anyway the magic always fades,

I will watch Fantasia three times in a row in wide eyed wonderment, chasing police cars on my bike always losing but the rush is always fun, I crave a simpler life one without the complication of a man to mess up my day so I will keep them at bay, tell them all to stay the fuck away.

The dying Dream

I refuse to gloss over the ugly truth that's something I could never do,

DR. King's dream it changed things for the best mostly,

But on the other side of the coin what it's done is make those that discriminate wear a mask and do it from the shadows, those are the clever ones,

But I still get those who turn down their nose ask me "What are you?" I say "human, how about you?" like it's any of their Goddamn business what race I am, but some people don't see faces they just see colour, and it knocks me sick,

We all came from the same primordial soup so what does it matter if we don't look the same obviously that's the way it was meant to be and those same hypocrites who complain about what they haven't got want to deny the next person of their human rights,

It isn't the 40's anymore but sometimes I think it may as well be, we may have a black president but even he isn't immune to mudslinging the white house is stained with it,

And when Katrina hit Bush didn't give a shit, I was stopped in Chicago airport and sent to customs and I was shocked to find the place filled with Muslims even children in tears, in their eyes I saw the fear,

When my anger subsided I knew I'd finally decided that the world is sick and there's no cure for it, what happened to the dream?

It's dying now is what it seems.

Most wonderful time of the year

If I hear one more jingle bell or see any more red and green I will literally scream,

These Christmas songs they're haunting me and I'm just about through,
You'll find no Christmas cheer over here dear so go ahead call me Scrooge, miserable and rude,

Because no incandescent tree is going to make my woes flee,

So excuse me if I don't pretend that on this one day of the year all of my problems disappear,

If Father Christmas is real will someone please tell him to get me the fuck up out of here because this is without a doubt the loneliest day of the year,

Baileys isn't strong enough to block any of this out we're all being too polite to scream and shout,

Let's paint smiles on our faces initiate fake warm embraces and pretend we aren't swimming in debt,

Let's all talk about what we've been blessed with omitting all the bad shit lying through our teeth I bet,

They say it's the most wonderful time of the year but I tend to disagree,

You all can go ahead and pretend but I think Christmas just isn't for me.

Wolves

Wolves in sheep's clothing I befriend because I find it fascinating,

Always one step ahead but act like my intuition is procrastinating,

I like change because routine I find mundane and so damn draining,

I travel and learn because as a child my teacher said I'd amount to nothing at all,

I'm not one to gloat but how I'd like to give that bitch a call,

I love my city I'm proud of my roots,

But I want to feel earth from every continent underneath my boots,

I'm so self-assured you'd think this was preinstalled,

But I worked hard for this confidence I struggled for many years,

I was lamb to the slaughter in my school days until I was bitten by wolves now I travel the world to be the person I'm supposed to be,

Whoever that boy is supposed to be.

Hearts beat

Oh it's funny, funny how good luck and the feeling of content runs out like monies spent,

Resulting in the arrangement of best friends, wine and a fruitful vent,

What's due is due who's to say when but I admit theses times are trying,

I'm Nonchalant but my calm aura is dying,

What a wasted summer I could have been anywhere spent my time with better people not mixed with those far below my equal,

And no that is not ego it's honesty something that seems to escape them but it's ok,

I mean I am I will shrug my shoulders and carry on as I am.

Hearts beat, they don't tick but I swear I hear ticking when I'm alone,

My resilience is running low, not sure if I can do this anymore, I swear this is transcendent,

Different face same damn situation,

I'm not saying I'm unhappy, I'm just not happy yet,

And the ticking is deafening.

Cherry tree

Remember when Moschino was the shit?

Remember how you wasn't it unless you rocked it?

Remember watching Nickelodeon on Saturday afternoons?

Copious amounts of Sister Sister rerun's,

Goldeneye and Mario Kart tournaments crowded around that tiny screen,

I'm pretty sure those days are the happiest I've ever been,

Everything was much more simple back then,

I wish those days didn't have to end,

Carefree, stress free nothing bothered me, I wasn't materialistic then I was easily pleased,

I didn't know about love, didn't care to explore it, so my heart was still intact no cracks within it,

Back when my dad was still around, I really miss him, that's why I'm wishing,

We could all revisit that time and I swear I'd appreciate it more, I wouldn't laugh at mum's Ugo,

I'd tell her how grateful I was that she was working so hard,

I wouldn't be rude I'd just be gleeful, how I wish those days didn't have to go,

Sitting under our Cherry tree dreaming of all I'd like to be,

Oh how I miss that version of me.

Time fool

Don't let time fool you,

Time can trick you into thinking you've forgotten,

It's a nasty circumstance its crude and damn right rotten,

Because when you hear that song or see that place it's like no time has passed at all,

You're back to that emotional space in a heartbeat,

It can happen so abruptly you'll be knocked right off your feet,

Please don't be gullible and let time fool you,

No matter what the old wives will adamantly say time is not a healer, remember that and you'll be ok.

This Grey City

This grey city it may not be pretty but it's the city that made me,

Notoriously gritty concealed by constant rain sent from the Gods to wash away the pain,

93' and the shootings were prominent I was young but I knew which estates to avoid,

Gunchester was what the news said two gangs and the police were the third young eyes in a dark adult world,

94' and everybody played Mary J 94' every street I smelt Mary Jane I'd climb our cherry tree every day and bathe in sunlight just to escape the hustle,

Two jobs my mother was never there to cuddle I guess those days shaped the person that I came to be ambitious and independent emotionally,

This grey city, the concrete rose if you're gonna survive stay on your toes, you better know the right people and be streetwise,

It's tough out there my city ain't pretty but I love it let the rain wash all your sins away ride out into the sunset like back in the day.

96' my first concert Snoop dog, half way through and it all kicked off, 10 and 11 the crowd lifted us to safety 20 men strong and the shit got crazy,

That year the IRA bomb went off in Piccadilly and it hit home that we were never really safe at all,

We moved to M21 and I felt like fresh prince, had my own room and my own Scaletrix,

We didn't need a card to pay our electric,

The crime began to eventually die down, inside I too got a little bit down, School wasn't what I thought it would turn out to be,

Some boys I guess just never would understand me but I guess that's just the way of my city.

Divine

No romantic plans in my day's plan so I send impending mundane thoughts
packing with a flippant shrug and a swift wave of my hand,

Cause I'm fine, in fact I'm due some free time,

So very sick of my expectations not being met or to be swept aside for some
other guy that's fine I guess right now's not my time,

They say those who wait for everything walk away with nothing so if that's
his choice what am I to say guess he'll realise his mistake one day,

But for me I will read and write, sing and pour some Sauvignon blanc
because you've just got to be good to yourself and people don't seem to do
that shit these days' people are just too needy to have these glorious lazy
days,

I'm not quite sure I want to open my door or answer my phone,

I guess for today I'd like the world to leave me alone,

I don't have to politely navigate my way around a fancy dinner plate smiling
politely trying to make the best impression,

No I don't have a date and that's more than fine with me I will devour pizza,
sip my wine and watch this film for the fourteenth time,

Yes, that would be divine

Safety pin (For Mum)

You keep me in check when I'm low you detect my issues that I can't blot away with tissues,

I think me as strong but compared to yours my strength is minute so when I crumble you build me back up like bricks prepare me for tests that are sure to come,

And though I feint like everything's great sometimes, you see through it all so when others take my words as fact swiftly turn their backs and go home to sleep you stick around just to say four words to me 'it will be ok' and coming from you that's all you'd need to say,

Because I know if I fall back you'll push me along if I stumble you'd make sure I wouldn't completely bail and tumble down,

Because just when I'm at that point where I'm about to fall apart you are there to keep me together you're my safety pin,

Some people think I carry too much baggage so they'd rather be friends when I'm at my height that version of me is all they want to meet because if I show signs that I'm on a decline emotionally they quickly flee,

Fair weather friends, forever spinning the rotating doors, I can barely keep track of who is here for the real me and who sticks around for the real life photo shopped version I tend to pretend to be,

It's so hard to see but when I am blinded you point out the obvious,

When parts of me flail you pull me together promise me that this is just temporary bad weather and then you push me back together and hold me there,

My safety pin never gives in,

And I know I am a hard load to carry but you don't complain you always seem merry,

I was a man-child who grew up too soon and now re-visit my childhood is all I want to do,

But you see through all they want you to believe you look past this mask into the very heart of me,

So just when I'm about to crack you hold my hand and lead me back on track.

Dreamer

They say that I'm a dreamer and think of me disparagingly because I believe in such things as hopes and dreams,

I will go wherever the wondering winds decide to take me,

I often get told I don't act my age because I'm a free spirit and I won't conform,

I won't settle down in one place for far too long, when I'm done, I'm done what's the use of clinging on,

I won't be satisfied until I've at least attempted all the things that as a boy I dreamed of doing,

Hold that against me but I assume it's deep seeded envy they wish they were as fearless as me so they look at me disapprovingly,

But the way I see it is you're only stumped by your own cowardice there's no limits to what you can do if you truly believe it,

So they can say whatever they want because I won't even hear, I'll be on a plane somewhere to a place I've never been.

Sad songs make me happy

I've been hurt for the thousandth time and this time I didn't even feel the
need to cry,

He said we'd probably get married in the future,

He could definitely see it,

Took one week for him to gain amnesia and fuck Tyrone,

Yeah he blew it,

Ice cream and Prosecco couldn't even shift these deep blues,

Left the country to foreign lands to escape all of the fools,

I'm not weak, certainly not petty, I'm not one for woe is me,

So believe me when I say I'm strong enough to admit I'm surprised to still
be here,

When a fleeting moment occurred when I really wasn't sure,

Deemed myself all out at sea destined to surely drown,

Until I crawled back to shore on all fours then I was just about sure,

The only thing to take me back to being happy is to not be happy at all,

Sad songs make me happy,

Depression I'm comfortable with,

Loneliness is my best friend,

Heartache I embrace till the end.

Dare to dream

Dare to dream,

I will dare to dream,

Though I am aware it's not as simple as it may seem,

But just you try me,

I won't let any opportunity just idly slip right by me,

Dare to feel,

I will dare to feel

Like I can achieve what isn't thought of me,

Travel to foreign lands across the seas, experience things many people have

never seen,

Dare to fear,

I have dared to be fearful,

for without fear there is no drive,

Without drive there is no urge to strive,

Dare to dream,

I will dare to dream,

It was never installed within me so as a child I whispered to myself quietly

that I can be all that I ever wanted to be.

To my head

Love me or hate I have no penitence for the in-between,

I will always be the same there will be no negotiating,

So if you're waiting for some kind of dramatic shift of character,

Please pull up a chair and enjoy my maniacal laughter,

Your opinion of me isn't the book I live my life by,

Nor is it even a chapter,

You're a footnote in my life,

Who reads the small print anyway?

So go ahead and love me or hate me just like I said,

No matter your opinion it never goes to my head.

Nina Simone

I don't care about you or him or her,

In fact, can you all just kindly disappear,

Don't tell me to smile,

It's my right to be down,

And down is where I'll stay until I decide I no longer want to be,

Black is my mood,

Blue is my shade,

So what?

Yes that's the best argument I have right now my wit went for a wonder,

He left me with my woes,

I'll listen to Nina she knows,

Nobody understands these feelings but Nina Simone.

Sleeping in the middle

1.40am alone in my bed sleeping in the middle the benefit of being single,

Friends say I should go out and mingle, jump back in the pool but the dating game doesn't tempt me right now it's boring and at times cruel,

I could try speed dating just for the comedy value but as funny as that sounds I just can't be arsed right now,

I could go out on the scene amidst the bitchy queens but I feel too old in those places I feel like asking for boys I. D's,

I don't know what it is with couple-types they act like being single is a disease like if you get to close to them it passes on like fleas,

People keep offering to set me up on blind dates but let's be honest now, how many things that are described as blind turn out to be a good thing?

I wish boys wouldn't buy me drinks it's not flattering at all I've got my own money in my pocket, so stop it, go back to where you were at and let's just leave it at that,

Some people break their back to be in love but I'll take it or leave it to be honest, it's just not what I crave,

This is where the couples all chime in that I've actually gone insane.

Morose boy

I'm only now beginning to escape the ways of being the sullen boy I used to be it's taken me awhile but now when I smile I truly mean it it's no longer a ploy to hide how I'm truly feeling,

I was a boy who didn't really understand I searched for answers but none came to hand,

For a short while I tried religion Granma would have been proud I talked to Jesus he didn't reply so I decided that church just wasn't for me,

When my sister asked me why, why did my dad get stolen away "I guess it was just his time" is all I could muster to say,

But inside I had the same questions but held it in through drastic measures,

Childhood memories haunt me daily but not always for the worst remembering funny times is a good healer of deep seated hurt,

I've written about this before but I just couldn't do him justice I figure I was holding back not wanting to admit to the fact that my scars run so deep they pierce the back of me,

Sometimes I cry so many tears I struggle to even see,

But I'm no longer the morose boy I once was and although yes I still cry it's not all the time,

After 16 years I can finally say I'm doing fine.

I will tell it

I feel a change in the wind it's calling my name I knew this day would come I put my heart on it,

I feel it drawing near and I'm ready for the embrace, I stand to my feet determination moulds my face,

My past I've done my best to forget I put it in a dark and faraway place,

The silver lining is here and it's oh so blinding I'm bathed in the mist of it and I shall not be budging,

And I'll tell it to the mountains and I'll tell it to the sea, I'll tell it to everybody who didn't believe in me,

Thank you to all of those who said I'd never amount to much you were my motivation you really made me step up,

Now I truly understand when they say success is the best revenge you can have because now when I see the doubters I can't help but to laugh,

I was once a shadow you could see right through me my presence wasn't easily noticed I blended in easily and so they thought I'd fade away but look at me today, I put my stamp on this earth I did I guess they were all wrong,

And I'll tell it to the clouds and I'll tell it to the trees, I'll tell it to all those people who didn't think I could achieve,

And I'll tell this to all of those people who are like how I used to be, people like to see you down so they can use you as a foot step to elevate themselves,

But just know soon they too will tumble and that's when you rise, look them dead in their eyes and tell them "watch me survive".

Frozen (Dedicated to Amy Winehouse)

My gut is twisted in knots forcing me to grasp for air,

Words they float to me but do not penetrate stay suspended mid-air,

I so very badly would like to cry, show some kind of emotion, but instead
I'm just frozen fear prevents me from being open,

Unaware of the outcome, daren't I turn on my phone for cutting reminders
that you're no longer here,

They fill me with anger what a stupid waste, what a damn shame, I barely
even know what else to say,

Fly away black winged angel and don't you dare look back,

I say this in whisper and my voice begins to crack,

This world wasn't meant for you, you were bigger than it, the pain of
wanting more from life got too much for you to bear and this thinking is
commonly shared you weren't alone,

But yet in other ways you were "the melodramas of your day delivered
blows" and so now the chapter of your life does begin to close,

Peace you'll find in bird land I'll be sure to meet you there in time.

Take me as I am

There is an ache right here that will not stir,

I'm avoiding mirrors succumbing to fear that in place of my reflection my demons will appear,

My eyes they burn but do not tear I'm too good at suppressing them I've practised for years,

The things I say in my head make me think of myself something awful I don't need any enemies I do the job for them with such ease forcing my own self to my knees,

I pick myself apart like some completed puzzle, leaving myself in a heap on the floor even more fucked up then before,

Having known that I am not too aesthetically appealing the fact that lately I've feared my personality leaves a lot to be desired makes me just want to fold and forget about it all,

When the penny dropped that maybe there's a reason I always end up alone it hit the floor with a force stronger than I've ever known,

If this is my fate, then why wait?

But still after all this bad will I have against myself there still is a tiny whisper that tells me I'm not all that bad,

No I'm not pretty like him, far from it,

I don't have his intellect, not close to it,

I may not be as humours but take me as I am, and I say this not just to everyone else I say this to myself. Nae x

CPSIA information can be obtained
at www.ICGtesting.com
Printed in the USA
LVOW04s0915080116
469677LV00026B/508/P